WEEKLY WR READER

EARLY LEARNING LIBRARY

Nature's Food Chains

What Sea Animals Eat

by Joanne Mattern

Reading consultant: Susan Nations, M.Ed.,
author/literacy coach/consultant

Science and curriculum consultant: Debra Voege, M.A.,
science and math curriculum resource teacher

Please visit our web site at: www.garethstevens.com
For a free color catalog describing Weekly Reader® Early Learning Library's list
of high-quality books, call 1-877-445-5824 (USA) or 1-800-387-3178 (Canada).
Weekly Reader® Early Learning Library's fax: (414) 336-0164.

Library of Congress Cataloging-in-Publication Data

Mattern, Joanne, 1963-
    What sea animals eat / by Joanne Mattern.
       p. cm. — (Nature's food chains)
    Includes bibliographical references and index.
    ISBN-10: 0-8368-6875-7 — ISBN-13: 978-0-8368-6875-3 (lib. bdg.)
    ISBN-10: 0-8368-6882-X — ISBN-13: 978-0-8368-6882-1 (softcover)
    1. Marine animals—Food—Juvenile literature. 2. Food chains (Ecology)—
Juvenile literature. I Title. II. Series: Mattern, Joanne, 1963- Nature's food chains.
    QL121.M32 2007
    591.77—dc22
                                      2006009355

This edition first published in 2007 by
Weekly Reader® Early Learning Library
A Member of the WRC Media Family of Companies
330 West Olive Street, Suite 100
Milwaukee, WI 53212 USA

Editor: Barbara Kiely Miller
Art direction: Tammy West
Cover design, page layout, and illustrations: Dave Kowalski
Picture research: Diane Laska-Swanke

Picture credits: Cover, title, © Doug Perrine/naturepl.com; p. 5 © Doug Perrine/SeaPics.com;
p. 7 © David Shale/naturepl.com; p. 9 © Rudie Kuiter/SeaPics.com; p. 11 © Mark Conlin/SeaPics.com;
p. 13 © Kike Calvo/V & W/SeaPics.com; p. 15 © Ralf Kiefner/SeaPics.com; p. 17 © Georgette Douwma/
naturepl.com; p. 19 © Bob Cranston/SeaPics.com

Printed in the United States of America

1 2 3 4 5 6 7 8 9 10 09 08 07 06

Note to Educators and Parents

Reading is such an exciting adventure for young children! They are beginning to integrate their oral language skills with written language. To encourage children along the path to early literacy, books must be colorful, engaging, and interesting; they should invite the young reader to explore both the print and the pictures.

The *Nature's Food Chains* series is designed to help children learn about the interrelationships between animals in a food chain. In each book, young readers will learn interesting facts about what animals eat in different habitats and how food chains are connected into food webs.

Each book is specially designed to support the young reader in the reading process. The familiar topics are appealing to young children and invite them to read — and reread — again and again. The full-color photographs and enhanced text further support the student during the reading process.

In addition to serving as wonderful picture books in schools, libraries, homes, and other places where children learn to love reading, these books are specifically intended to be read within an instructional guided reading group. This small group setting allows beginning readers to work with a fluent adult model as they make meaning from the text. After children develop fluency with the text and content, the book can be read independently. Children and adults alike will find these books supportive, engaging, and fun!

— Susan Nations, M.Ed., author, literacy coach, and consultant in literacy development

All living things need food to live and grow. Some animals eat plants. Some eat smaller animals. These fish belong to a sea food chain. A **food chain** shows the order of who eats what.

Plants are at the bottom of food chains. They make their own food from sunshine, water, and air. These small shrimp eat tiny sea plants called **plankton**.

FOOD CHAIN

Shrimp

Plankton

Small fish eat the shrimp. **Seahorses** are fish. A seahorse eats this tiny shrimp.

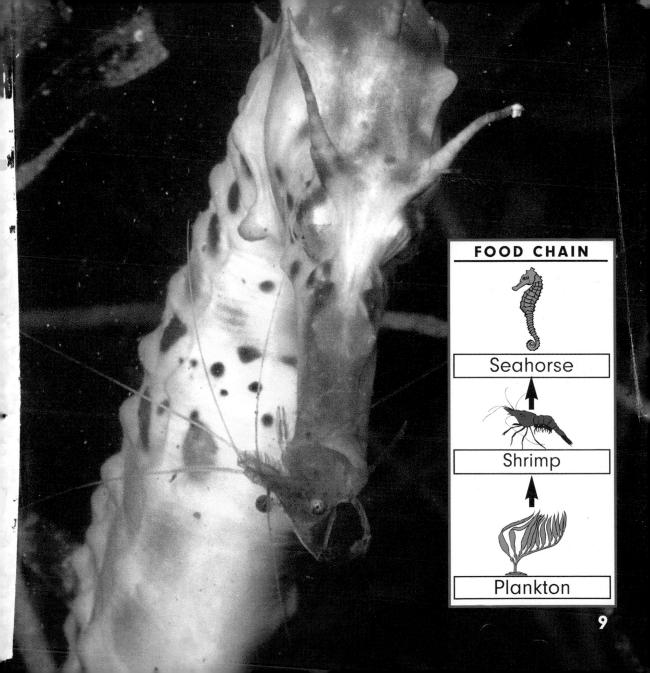

FOOD CHAIN

Seahorse

↑

Shrimp

↑

Plankton

Bigger fish eat seahorses.

These tuna eat seahorses.

FOOD CHAIN

Tuna

Seahorse

Shrimp

Plankton

Then a larger fish may eat the tuna.
This shark is eating a tuna. A shark
is a very big fish. Sharks are at the
top of their food chains. No other
sea animal will eat them.

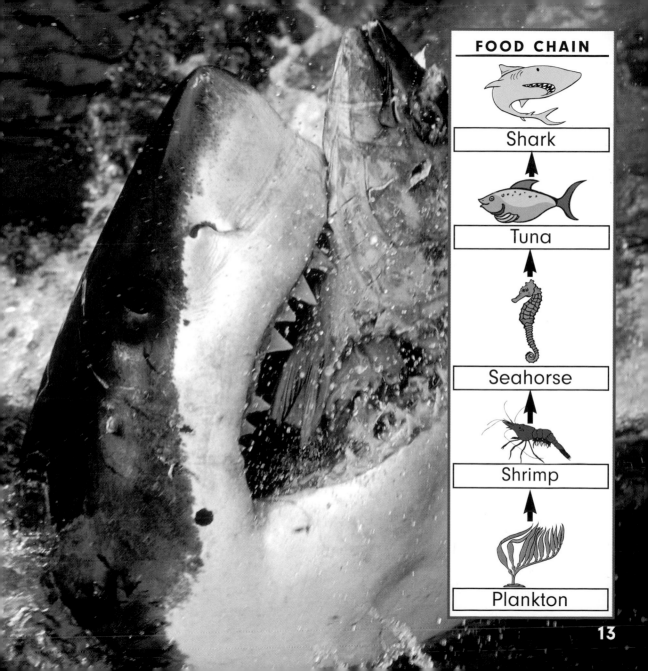

FOOD CHAIN

Shark

↑

Tuna

↑

Seahorse

↑

Shrimp

↑

Plankton

Oceans and seas have many food chains. A tuna ate the seahorse in the first food chain. But seahorses are also eaten by **crabs**.

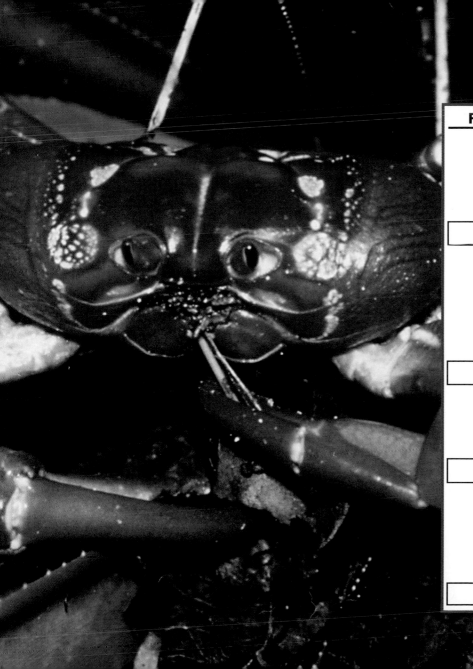

FOOD CHAIN

Crab

Seahorse

Shrimp

Plankton

15

Bigger animals eat crabs. This **squid** eats crabs. Then a shark eats the squid. The shark is at the top of this food chain, too.

FOOD CHAIN

Shark

↑

Squid

↑

Crab

An animal or plant can be part of more than one food chain. Sharks eat tuna and squid. This shark may eat crabs, but it eats plankton, too. Eating many kinds of foods helps animals stay alive.

A **food web** is formed when two or more food chains are connected. Animals that are part of more than one food chain connect the chains. Food webs show that animals have many things to eat!

A Sea Food Web

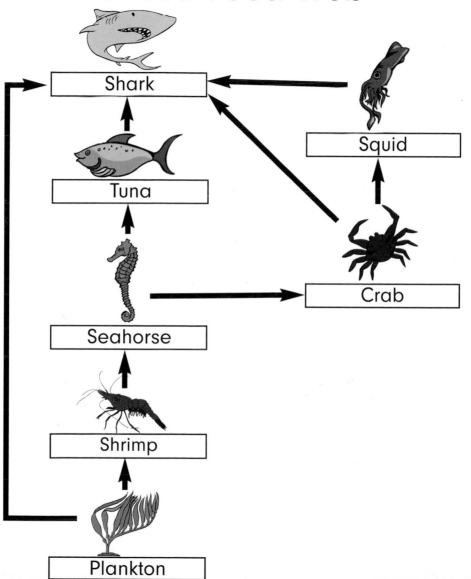

Glossary

crab — a water animal that has a hard shell and a pair of large claws

food chain — a list of living things, in which each plant or animal is eaten by the next animal on the list

food web — food chains that are connected by a plant or animal that is common to both chains

squid — a sea animal that is related to the octopus. A squid has a long, soft body and ten long arms.

For More Information

Books

Ocean Floors. Water Habitats (series). JoAnn Early Macken
(Gareth Stevens)

Seahorses. Sylvia M. James (Mondo Publishing)

Sharks. Scary Creatures (series). Penny Clarke
(Franklin Watts)

What Do Sharks Eat for Dinner? Scholastic Question
and Answer Books (series). Melvin Berger
(Scholastic Reference)

Web Site

Ocean Link
oceanlink.island.net/oinfo/foodweb/foodweb.html
Learn more about food webs for different ocean animals.

Index

About the Author

Joanne Mattern has written more than one hundred and fifty books for children. Joanne also works in her local library. She lives in New York State with her husband, three daughters, and assorted pets. She enjoys animals, music, going to baseball games, reading, and visiting schools to talk about her books.